Y0-CDP-529

Animals of Asia

LEVEL · READING LEVEL 2 GRADES 1 TO 3 · READER

Written by Kathryn Knight
Art Copyright © Edizioni Larus S.p.A.

Mountains of Asia

Asia's mountains are home to animals that live nowhere else on Earth. Snow leopards prowl the Himalayas (Him-oh-**lay**-uhs). Yaks and wild goats, such as the tahr (tar) and markhor (**mar**-core), live in high, cold lands. Bears and monkeys live on the slopes.

The rainy bamboo forests of the Chinese mountains are home to one of the rarest animals in Asia: the giant panda.

Himalayan Tahr

Red Panda

Silver Pheasant

Markhor

Giant Panda

Golden Pheasant

Common Pheasant

Giant Panda

The giant panda is very similar to a bear. It is about 5 feet long. It tends to live quietly alone, not in groups, in the mountains of southwestern China. It eats bamboo—up to 45 pounds of shoots and stems each day! Giant pandas are excellent climbers.

Newborn giant pandas are blind and deaf.
They are only 4 inches long at birth. The mother
feeds her cub with her milk for seven months,
until the young panda can eat bamboo on its
own. The cub will stay with its mother for
three years.

Red Panda

The red panda is about the size of a raccoon. Its rusty-red fur is soft, thick, and warm. It spends most of the day in the treetops. When it rests, it uses its long bushy tail as a pillow.

Manul

The manul looks like a pet cat, but it's a wild animal. It is a skilled hunter. Once it has spotted a rodent, lizard, or bird, it advances slowly—like a snake. Then it pounces and catches its meal.

Asiatic Black Bear

The Asiatic black bear climbs trees with its short, curved claws. It eats nuts, berries, insects, slugs, and snails. It also licks tree sap. This clever bear can build a platform in the trees using twigs and broken branches.

Yak

The yak is a form of wild ox. Yaks live in the highest, coldest places on Earth. Their thick, waterproof coats protect them in blizzards and temperatures of −40° F.

Northern and Central Asia

Asia has high mountains, but it also has forests, grasslands, and deserts. Just south of the frozen land of the Arctic region is the taiga (**ty**-guh), the largest forest in the world. The southeastern forests are home to the magnificent Siberian tiger.

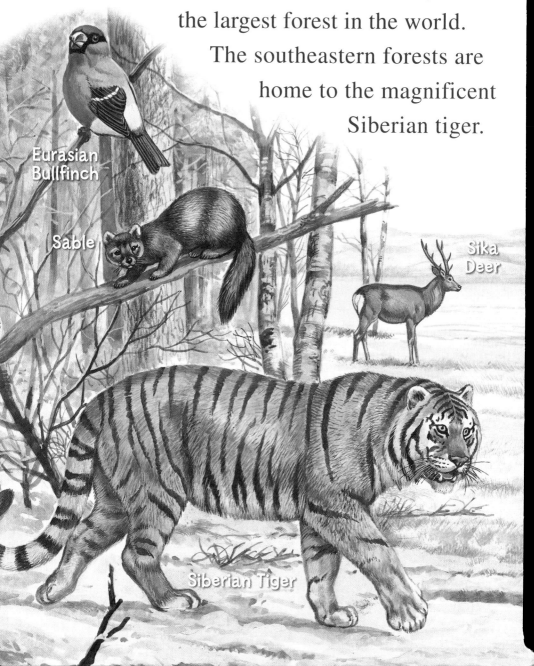

Eurasian Bullfinch

Sable

Sika Deer

Siberian Tiger

The grassland areas of central Asia are called the steppe (step). The dry lands are deserts. Herds of wild horses once raced across the steppe of Asia. The desert areas are home to rodents and camels.

Whooper Swan

Bactrian Camel

Reindeer

Przewalski's Horse

Francolin

Wolverine

Wolverine

The wolverine is the largest member of the weasel family. It has short, powerful legs and sharp claws. It eats berries, rodents, birds, eggs, foxes, and even reindeer.

Wolverines will challenge other animals fiercely. They let out a smell that is so awful that animals flee. In fact, the wolverine's nickname is "skunk bear."

Reindeer

The small reindeer lives in herds in the northern taiga. It can run on its short, sturdy legs for hours. Its thick coat keeps it warm. Reindeer have antlers up to 4 feet long!

Saiga

The saiga (**sy**-guh) has quick, slender legs and can sprint 50 miles an hour over the steppe. Its snout is very unusual. At the tip is a movable trunk!

Southern Asia

The warm, tropical areas of southern Asia are rainy and wet. In the jungles and forests here, monkeys scamper from tree to tree. Beautiful birds grace the air. The dry, open, grassy areas are called the savanna. Animals may *migrate* (move with the seasons) between the forest and the savanna.

Asian Elephant

Bengal Tiger

Chital

The most handsome predator of the savanna is the Bengal tiger, known as the "royal tiger." Males are about 10 feet long and can weigh up to 600 pounds!

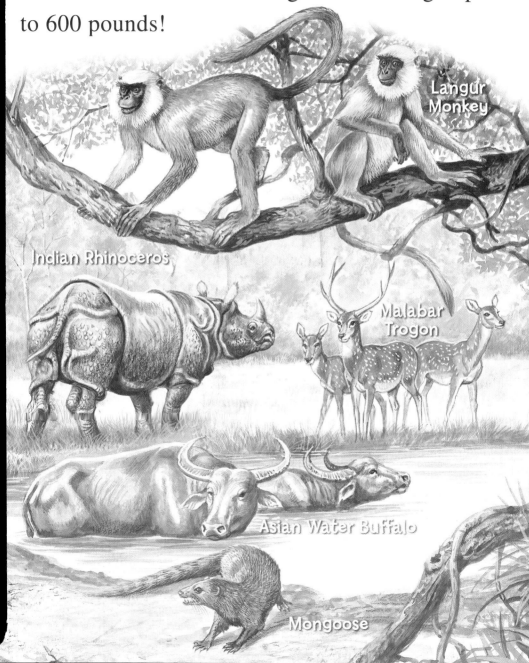

Langur Monkey

Indian Rhinoceros

Malabar Trogon

Asian Water Buffalo

Mongoose

Asian Elephant

Majestic Asian elephants can weigh five tons. They eat 200 pounds of grass and leaves a day. Their ears are smaller than the ears of the African elephant. Only a few males have tusks.

Asian elephants have a gentle nature. They adapt well to humans and are often used as work animals.

Indian Rhinoceros

   The powerful Indian rhinoceros can weigh 4,000 pounds. It has thick, armor-like skin. The rhino's horn can grow a foot long. It is not made of bone. It's made of *keratin* (fibers like those in your hair and fingernails). To stay cool, a rhinoceros may spend eight hours a day soaking in pools of water and mud.

Malayan Tapir

The odd-looking tapir (**tay**-per) of the tropical forest is 8 feet long. It is stocky, like a pig, and is a good swimmer. It uses its small trunk to pluck plants to eat. The tapir is shy and timid, but it will screech, snort, and bite to defend itself.

The sloth bear has sharp, curved claws (like the claws of a sloth) and a long sticky tongue. It loves fruit, flowers, sugarcane, and termites. When it finds a termite nest, it tears a hole in the walls with its tough claws. Then it sticks in its snout and sucks up the little insects.

Mongoose

The Indian gray mongoose is famous for being a snake killer. It can leap and change direction quickly and run backward! It can out-move the darting head of a cobra.

Mongooses are playful, curious animals and are easy to tame. They groom their thick fur by smoothing and combing it.

King Cobra

The king cobra is the longest poisonous snake, reaching over 18 feet. It widens its neck skin into a "hood" to scare animals. When it strikes, it hisses loudly. The king cobra's sharp teeth inject *venom* (poison) into its victim. This venom can kill a human in fifteen minutes—but it has little effect on a mongoose.

The rivers and wetlands of southern Asia are home to many amazing animals. The gharial (**gur**-ee-uhl) has a long, thin snout. It feeds on fish. The archerfish can spit water to knock an insect off a water plant!

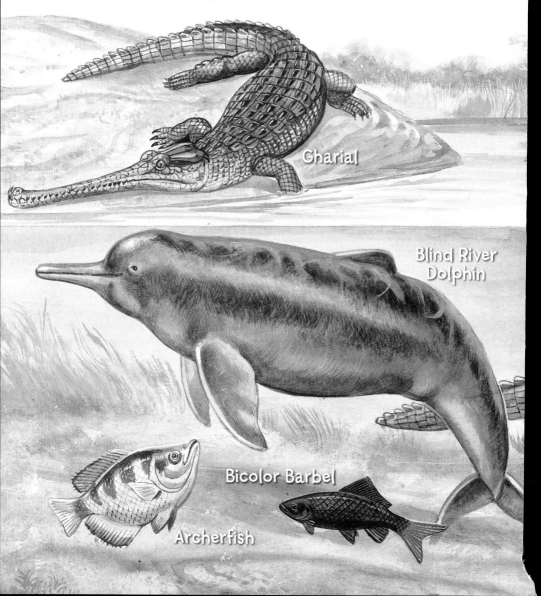

Gharial

Blind River Dolphin

Bicolor Barbel

Archerfish

The blind river dolphin is very, very rare. The sultan has colorful feathers—but is good at hiding!

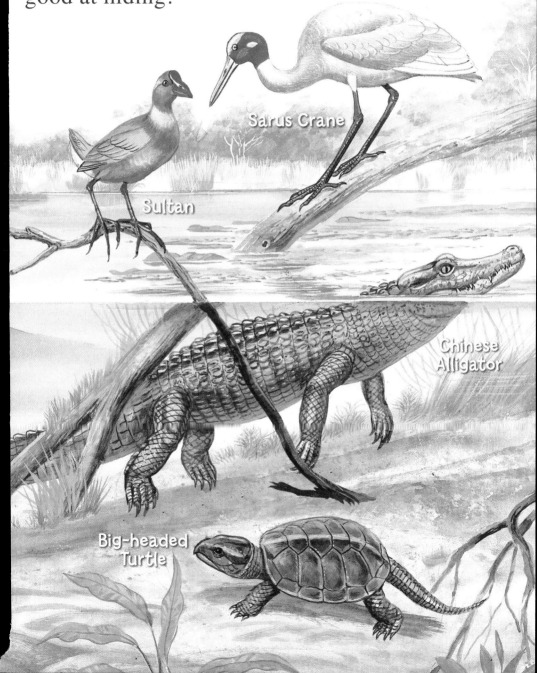

Sarus Crane

Sultan

Chinese Alligator

Big-headed Turtle

The Forests of Southern Asia

The warm forests of southern Asia are alive with surprising animals. The orangutan is the largest Asian ape. The proboscis (pro-**boss**-kiss) monkey has a long, odd nose. The babirusa (bab-uh-**roo**-suh) is also called a pig-deer. And this area is home to a dragon! The huge Komodo dragon lives on a small island. It is 10 feet long— the largest lizard in the world!

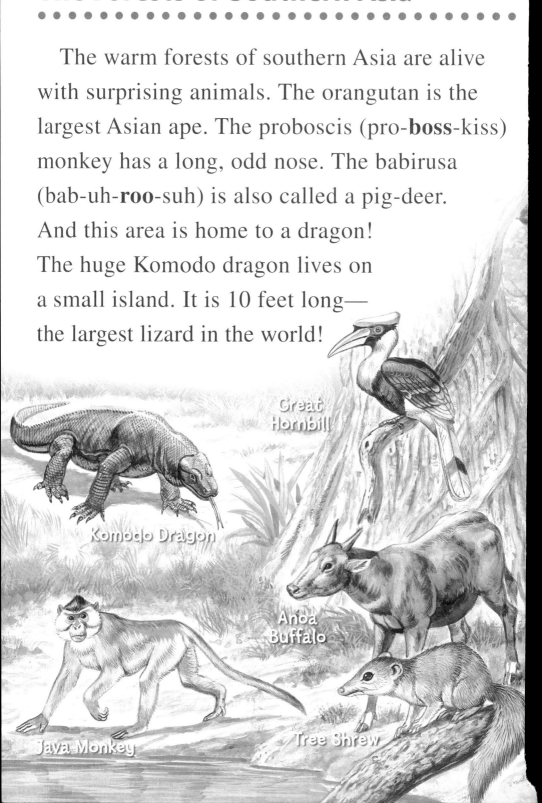

Great Hornbill

Komodo Dragon

Anoa Buffalo

Java Monkey

Tree Shrew

Slender Loris (Sloth Monkey)

The slender loris has large eyes that see well in the dark. It spends the day sleeping, and when night falls, it goes in search of food.

Tarsier (Specter-lemur)

The tarsier (**tar**-see-er) also has large eyes, and it can move its head in any direction. It leaps from branch to branch, looking for insects or lizards to eat.